To: Nohemy

From: Kim

Christmas 2003

"I know the plans I have for you," declares the LORD,

"plans to prosper you and not to harm you,

plans to give you hope and a future."

JEREMIAH 29:11

Written & Compiled by Sarah M. Hupp
Associate Editor: Molly C. Detweiler

Printed in China
03 04/HK/ 7 6 5 4

God Always Has a Plan B

for women

CONTENTS

6
God Gives Second Chances
(And Sometimes Third & Fourth & ...)

18
Failure is One of God's Teachers

32
Messed Up? Ask God to Clean It Up!

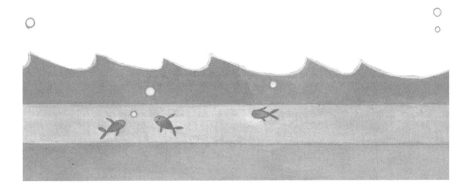

56
Feeling Out of Control? God's in Control!

90
Nobody's Perfect (Whew!)

108
All Things Work Together for the Good ... Really!

138
Stressed Spelled Backward Is Desserts!

GOD GIVES SECOND CHANCES (AND SOMETIMES THIRD & FOURTH & ...)

The Grace of a Second Chance

Ninth-grade algebra class was my all-time favorite. Because I loved puzzles, algebra was actually fun. In math class, I faced each test with confidence! Tuesday's test would be no different.

But while taking the test, I suddenly found that I couldn't remember the formula for number one ... number two, or three, four, five ... I had gone blank! I could solve only the last two problems. Stunned, I handed my paper to the teacher. After a long pensive pause, she asked, "When do you have study hall tomorrow?" "At ten," I nervously replied. The next day at ten sharp, I was sitting in my algebra classroom with a second chance. I was given a gift called "grace."

God is a God of grace who not only saves you from eternal death but also saves you from a defeated life. If you focus only on what it's like to fail in certain areas of your life, you could be drawn into the downward spiral of dejection. However, how blessed you are to know the God of grace who saves you from your failures. He is the God of the second chance ... and the third ... and the fourth ...

June Hunt

Amazing grace! how sweet the sound,
That saved a wretch like me;
I once was lost, but now I'm found;
Was blind, but now I see.

JOHN NEWTON

Here is a trustworthy saying that deserves full acceptance:
Christ Jesus came into the world to save sinners—of whom
I am the worst. But for that very reason I was shown mercy
so that in me, the worst of sinners, Christ Jesus might display
his unlimited patience as an example for those who
would believe on him and receive eternal life.

1 TIMOTHY 1:15–16

I Need a "Do-Over"!

The church picnic had been full of fun and fellowship, and now it was time for some spirited competition. Willing participants teamed up on either side of a hastily erected volleyball net. Non-athletes and wiggly toddlers found places for lawn chairs and blankets around the court's perimeter. As the game began, a novice teen attempted a serve from the back of the volleyball court, but her effort fell short. The volleyball smacked soundly into the net.

"Do over! I need a 'do-over,'" the teen bawled. Her teammates loudly agreed, but the other players protested. The pastor solved the dispute by suggesting that each player on each team would be allowed to call one "do-over" during the course of the game.

"After all," the pastor declared, "God willingly gives us second chances. Those "do-overs" are often life changing, too. However, even though God is gracious and forgives over and over again, this game's only going to give you *one* second chance."

With lots of laughter the game continued, and it was a close one. Yet teammates and toddlers alike learned a lesson amidst the fun that day—God allows "do-overs" —sometimes in church picnic volleyball games, but more importantly in life, too.

Sarah Hupp

A New Leaf

He came to my desk with quivering lip—
 The lesson was done.
"Dear Teacher, I want a new leaf," he said,
 "I have spoiled this one."
I took the old leaf, stained and blotted,
And gave him a new one all unspotted,
 And into his sad eyes smiled,
 "Do better, now, my child."

I went to the throne with a quivering soul—
 The old year was done.
"Dear Father, have you a new leaf for me?
 I have spoiled this one."
He took the old leaf, stained and blotted,
And gave me a new one all unspotted,
 And into my sad heart smiled,
 "Do better, now, my child."

KATHLEEN WHEELER

Miriam's Reprieve

Aging Miriam, Moses' sister and a leader to the wandering Hebrews, stepped outside the boundaries by usurping God's authority. So she was struck with leprosy and cast out of the camp. There Miriam, the once revered leader, sat with a withered body. The angst of Miriam's heart, the humiliation of her circumstances, must have flooded her with fear. Separated from everything and everyone she loved, Miriam huddled in her personal agony.

My heart aches when I read of Miriam, for I know what it's like to feel like an outcast. But, when we get to the end of ourselves, behold: there, at the threshold of change, is God's love that has no fear of the leper in us.

In both Miriam's story and mine we experience an invitation back into the camp. The Lord longs for our return. While Scripture serves as a life-map for us, God's fearless love acts as a safety net to catch us and then to infuse us with the courage to try again and again and again.

Patsy Clairmont

December's Story

In her early teens, a pastor's daughter named December rebelled. And then she ran away. "By the time I was seventeen, I was a homeless teen who slept in my parked car on the streets of San Jose," she said. She was desperately looking for some kind of affirmation, some kind of love without conditions and rules.

Eventually her looking for love in all the wrong places left her alone—and pregnant. "When I told the baby's father I was pregnant, he walked out of my life. I sinned a lot, but I couldn't bring myself to abort this baby."

And then she walked an even more precarious tightrope—needing her family, yet feeling like she had embarrassed her father; needing the church, but feeling like an outcast. "I just knew they wouldn't forgive me."

Eventually, knowing her parents and church members would find out about her pregnancy, she knew she "had to face Mom and Dad."

The next Monday December met her parents in her dad's church office. Her hands trembled. She just knew that what she was about to tell them would destroy their ministry and crush their last hope for her.

"This morning I need a parent, not a pastor," she started.

But before she could finish, her dad interrupted: "I already know you're pregnant, Dee," he said.

After a short silence, December began to weep. Her parents drew near and hugged her close. Her mom broke the awkward silence, speaking just the right words at just the right time: "You'd better eat something, Dee. You've got to nourish our baby."

As Dee turned to God, she sensed his forgiveness. As she returned to her family, they sensed God directing them to welcome her. She told me, "The bottom line is that I came back to my family and God because they loved me with no strings attached. They forgave me. I knew they cared. I thought I could do something to make them disown me, but I was wrong."

Chonda Pierce

*Be strong and courageous, and do the work. Do not
be afraid or discouraged, for the LORD God, my God,
is with you. He will not fail you or forsake you.*

1 CHRONICLES 28:20

*God's mercy extends to those who fear him,
from generation to generation.*

LUKE 1:50

*This I call to mind
    and therefore I have hope:
Because of the LORD's great love we are not consumed,
    for his compassions never fail.
They are new every morning;
    great is your faithfulness.*

LAMENTATIONS 3:21–23

I look not back—God knows the fruitless efforts,
The wasted hours, the sinning and regrets;
I leave them all with Him that blots the record,
And graciously forgives, and then forgets.

Annie Johnson Flint

I do not know how the Spirit of Christ performs it, but he brings us choices through which we never-endingly change, fresh and new, into his likeness.

Joni Eareckson Tada

From inside the fish Jonah prayed to the LORD his God. He said:

> *"In my distress I called to the LORD,*
>> *and he answered me.*
> *From the depths of the grave I called for help,*
>> *and you listened to my cry.*
> *You hurled me into the deep,*
>> *into the very heart of the seas,*
>> *and the currents swirled about me;*
> *all your waves and breakers*
>> *swept over me. . . .*
> *But I, with a song of thanksgiving,*
>> *will sacrifice to you.*
> *What I have vowed I will make good.*
>> *Salvation comes from the LORD."*

And the LORD commanded the fish, and it vomited Jonah onto dry land. Then the word of the LORD came to Jonah a second time: "Go to the great city of Nineveh and proclaim to it the message I give you." Jonah obeyed the word of the LORD and went to Nineveh.

JONAH 2:1–3, 9—3:3

Another Chance

Since the time of our first father and mother our God has offered another chance to those who have failed. Many who thought they had flunked out of life for good reentered and graduated with honors. History tells of those who learned from their failures and became successful. Jonah was one. After he learned the lessons of failure, God gave him another chance.

The far side of the sea—that's where Jonah had headed to escape God's command. Yet, after God commanded the fish to deposit Jonah on land, "the word of the LORD came to Jonah a second time" (Jonah 3:1). A second time to Jonah—and to Moses, and to Samson, and to David, and to Peter, and to John Mark. And, using our sin, our failure, as a great teacher, the word of the Lord also comes to us a second time, offering another chance.

We have a God of the second chance. He recycles our failures, using them for his purposes. And our failure can be the best preparation for our conformity to the image of Christ if we submit to its lessons while we wait for another chance.

Elisa Morgan

FAILURE IS ONE OF GOD'S TEACHERS

Sloppy Living

A number of years ago Jim Bakker's ministry collapsed under a barrage of accusations that ultimately landed him in prison. Jim's jail time led him from suicidal despair to repentance, victory, and, once again, ministry. Bakker maintains that the horror of his public humiliation, conviction, and incarceration was the best thing that ever happened to him. Through it all, Jim experienced the Father's refusal to let sloppy living take precedence over the call to obedience. Jim learned the hard way, but in the learning he was held safely in the grip of his Father's sustaining grace.

God our Father keeps tabs on us and "won't let us get by" with living at a level below that to which he calls us. At some point, something or someone will come along as an instrument of God's love and discipline to lead us back to obedience. Never during that process is God's grace exhausted or his love extinguished. He simply manipulates our circumstances in such a way that our attention and direction are drawn back toward him. That knowledge of his steadfast commitment to keep us ultimately "on track" makes us feel secure ... and keeps us safe.

Marilyn Meberg

We do not have a high priest who is unable to sympathize with our weaknesses, but we have one who has been tempted in every way, just as we are—yet was without sin. Let us then approach the throne of grace with confidence, so that we may receive mercy and find grace to help us in our time of need.

HEBREWS 4:15–16

We do not lose heart. Though outwardly we are wasting away, yet inwardly we are being renewed day by day. For our light and momentary troubles are achieving for us an eternal glory that far outweighs them all.

2 CORINTHIANS 4:16–17

The Deserter

A famous evangelist was looking for a "go getter" to serve on his team. John had the skills. He had been active in his home church, too, so the job was his. What an opportunity! John was excited!

Then reality hit. No Hilton Hotels, no chauffeured limousines. The entire crusade was a struggle. Opposition from all sides. People threatening his life. This wasn't what John had in mind. So, John deserted. Took his bedroll. Left the team.

Though called apart to serve with the apostle Paul on his first missionary journey, John, also called Mark, failed big time. He failed so badly that Paul adamantly refused John's cousin Barnabas's suggestion to take John Mark along on another missionary trip, citing John's desertion as a reason to leave the boy at home (Acts 12–13, 15).

But God didn't hold John Mark's failure against him. Eleven years later, Scripture records that God's grace restored the relationship between Paul and John Mark. The dispirited deserter became a faithful fellow worker to the apostle (Colossians 4:10–11), useful to Paul's ministry and a joy to Paul's heart (2 Timothy 4:11).

If God can mend John Mark's misstep, can he forgive your failure, too? You betcha! Just ask.

Sarah Hupp

Flapping Flight

We all have days of flapping flight as we struggle to find our customized, God-ordained niche. And just when we think we've found it, he gives us a glimpse of another challenge. Will we stay in the "comfort zone" or will we move into "the risk zone"? More than a few times I have failed, "flapped," and tried again. With each success comes greater confidence.

It is not essential that other people validate our success. It's encouraging when they do, but it is not what's ultimately important. When we walk in obedience and fix our minds on truth, our disappointments will eventually produce passions that will result in actions that are honorable and holy. *That's when we soar on wings like eagles!*

Carol Kent

Celebrating Failure

The Ore-Ida frozen potato company celebrates anniversaries of failure (They're the folks who make frozen cauliflower, broccoli, mushrooms, French fries, etc., and they're famous for innovative, creative ideas.) What do they do when one of those ideas bombs? Do they blame or fire somebody? No, they throw a party! Literally. A cannon is fired and everybody stops work to commemorate the "perfect failure." Together they rejoice in what they've learned. They talk about what will not work, reveling in the fact that no more time, energy, or money has to be spent on a thankless project.

You see, *nothing* in our lives is wasted. Not one thing that happens is without worth somewhere down the road. But we often miss it because we "travel the beaten path" and fail to open our eyes to the outlandish ways God wants to speak to us and love us and change us. We don't recognize the value in celebrating the strange twists, the difficulties, the so-called failures, when we really should ... and could. We consider our flops or hard times a defeat, but in reality they are God's greatest compliments. They're transforming love gifts from a gracious heavenly Father.

Luci Swindoll

My help comes from the LORD,
the Maker of heaven and earth.
He will not let your foot slip.

PSALM 121:2–3

Let nothing move you. Always give yourselves fully
to the work of the Lord, because you know that your
labor in the Lord is not in vain.

1 CORINTHIANS 15:58

My flesh and my heart may fail,
but God is the strength of my heart
and my portion forever.

PSALM 73:26

Success is never permanent. Failures are never final. The only thing that counts is to never, ever give up.

Author Unknown

The God of spring's new life, of summer's joy and of autumn's fullness is also the God of winter's chill. Although we never know what lies buried beneath the frozen stillness, we can trust that surely, surely, after winter comes the spring.

Debra Klingsporn

Even in the uttermost depths of the darkness,
I see before me your light of hope,
 your light of faith,
 and your light of love
 burning deep within me,
Giving me
 an unspeakable,
 peaceful,
 assurance,
knowing you will perform
what you have spoken.

KATHY TROCCOLI

Count the Cost

On an afternoon drive, my husband and I spotted a handmade "For Sale" sign propped up beside an immense house. A potholed drive wound past rotting building supplies and piles of dried concrete. Missing its front doors and most of its windows, the three-story dwelling resembled a ghostly jack-o-lantern. The chimney was unfinished; shingles covered only one face of the roof. Only one room in the large house was habitable. Clearly someone had miscalculated the total cost of building this mansion. The materials, time and money that had been invested were wasting away in the rain and wind. Hoping to recoup their losses, the owners had listed the home for sale.

We all make mistakes, underestimate, or fall short in this life. Sometimes those blunders are visible, like the partially constructed mansion. But sometimes our missteps are inner failings of the heart, known only to ourselves and God. These mistakes can damage our relationships with others and God.

The best way to recoup these kinds of losses is to surrender our hearts to God's care. He alone knows the cost of building the mansion of our lives from beginning to end. And he will take into account every brick, shingle, and nail to get the job done right.

Sarah Hupp

*[Trials] have come so that your faith—of greater worth
than gold, which perishes even though refined by fire—
may be proved genuine and may result in praise, glory and
honor when Jesus Christ is revealed.*

1 PETER 1:7

*All have sinned and fall short of the glory of God and
are justified freely by his grace through the redemption
that came by Christ Jesus.*

ROMANS 3:23–24

*[The Lord] said to me, "My grace is sufficient for you,
for my power is made perfect in weakness." Therefore I will
boast all the more gladly about my weaknesses, so that Christ's
power may rest on me. That is why, for Christ's sake, I delight in
weaknesses, in insults, in hardships, in persecutions, in
difficulties. For when I am weak, then I am strong.*

2 CORINTHIANS 12:9–10

The Downhill Twins

Discouragement and disappointment are like twins. Open the door to disappointment, and you will find discouragement dashing in right behind. And once discouragement enters your camp, it seems to be downhill all the way.

That is why God was so careful in his instructions to Joshua as the Israelites prepared to occupy the land that God had given them. Joshua knew the results of discouragement. He and Caleb had torn their clothes, beseeching the children of Israel to walk in faith, to believe God (Numbers 13:30). Yet they would not listen. Word of the giants and the fortified cities had penetrated their line of defense, and discouragement followed, bringing dejection and despair.

So what is God's word to you today? It is to be strong and courageous, for your Father, the Lord God Omnipotent, reigns. Rejoice in the God of your salvation, for he is your strength and he will enable you to stand (Habakkuk 3:18–19).

Kay Arthur

Our Finest Teacher

In the New Testament we have the joy of listening in as the seeker, the lost, the broken, the forgotten, the paralyzed, and the skeptical gather around Jesus. The Lord, who understood their frayed and scattered condition, prescribed truth, direction, wholeness, mercy, forgiveness, love, and liberty for all who came with an ear to hear and a heart to receive.

Interestingly, the ones who were the most receptive were the most obviously damaged (lepers, crippled, grief-stricken, neglected). That confirms what I've always suspected: The things we fear (pain, failure, disgrace, rejection, limitations) are ultimately some of our finest teachers, educating us in compassion, grace, wisdom, and understanding.

I love the chorus, "Turn your eyes upon Jesus, look full in his wonderful face, and the things of earth will grow strangely dim in the light of his glory and grace." And that, my friend, includes our fears. They will wither in his presence while we grow in grace.

Patsy Clairmont

God's Gift

Our gracious God offers us all tenderness and pardon. We step through our lives, fail to consider the consequences of what we're about to do, and spit our selfish desires in the face of Jesus. Once we realize what we've done, we begin to plead for mercy and forgiveness. Even though he's hurt and grieved about what we've done, he listens to our plea, wraps us in his loving embrace, and grants us unmerited favor—grace that is greater than all our sin.

Do you need pardon and reconciliation? Amazing grace is the kind of grace we sing about. It is yours for the unwrapping. Accept the gift. Open it with joy!

Thelma Wells

MESSED UP? ASK GOD TO CLEAN IT UP!

"Come now, let us reason together,"
  says the LORD.
"Though your sins are like scarlet,
  they shall be as white as snow;
though they are red as crimson,
  they shall be like wool."

ISAIAH 1:18

Let us draw near to God with a sincere heart in full assurance
of faith, having our hearts sprinkled to cleanse us from a guilty
conscience and having our bodies washed with pure water.

HEBREWS 10:22

If we confess our sins, he is faithful and just and will forgive
us our sins and purify us from all unrighteousness.

1 JOHN 1:9

God's Embrace

Knowing that God's Son died so that I can have an intimate relationship with the Almighty makes me want to reach out my short, chubby arms, grab Jesus around his neck, and hug him the way my grandchildren hug me tight and say, "Grammy, I love you!" Even when they've misbehaved, they can come to me and steal my heart with their sweet embrace.

When we embrace the grace of God, we can come to him with the spirit of a little child and say, "Father, I've messed up. Please forgive me. I love you!" Instantly, faster than a grandmother's pardon, God grants us his unmerited favor through Christ Jesus and loves us freely once more.

What a gift! When you mess up, God's there to clean you up. Just run to him with your arms open wide. He'll return your embrace every time.

Thelma Wells

The Greatest Artist

Some fishermen in the highlands of Scotland came into a little Scottish inn late one afternoon for a cup of tea. As one was describing "the one that got away" to his friends, he flung out his hands in the typical fisherman's gesture. He did so just as the waitress was setting down his cup of tea. The resulting collision left a huge tea stain spreading on the whitewashed wall. The fisherman apologized profusely.

Another gentleman seated nearby said, "Never mind." Rising, he took a crayon from his pocket and began to sketch around the ugly brown stain. Slowly there emerged the head of a magnificent royal stag with antlers spread. The man was Sir Edwin Henry Landseer, England's foremost painter of animals.

Now if an artist can do that with an ugly brown stain, what can God do with my sins and mistakes if I but give them to him?

Ruth Bell Graham

It's so easy to look back on past mistakes, such as those I made while raising my children. When an older relative criticized my maternal efforts, anger hitchhiked along with guilt. For years, these destructive emotions kept me from a closer walk with God. But what a lesson Paul teaches me! He refused to dwell on past ugly mistakes or unfair criticism. He put those things behind him, and kept his eye on what was ahead, saying, "I press on toward the goal to win the prize for which God has called me heavenward in Christ Jesus" (Philippians 3:14).

Shirley Pope Waite

Should you encounter bad news today, look within yourself. You'll find God's Spirit, which will enable you to accept graciously that which has been handed to you.

Luci Swindoll

Cast your cares on the LORD and
he will sustain you;
he will never let the righteous fall.
PSALM 55:22

With God we will gain the victory.
PSALM 60:12

Even though I walk
through the valley of the shadow of death,
I will fear no evil, Lord,
for you are with me;
your rod and your staff,
they comfort me.
PSALM 23:4

Prayers From the Imperfect

When we admit to the core of our being that our performance will never measure up to God's standard, then we can quit trying to make ourselves good enough and concentrate instead on having a *relationship* with him. Everything, absolutely everything—from my tendency to be selfish to why the snails won't leave my potted plants alone—is acceptable to talk to him about. And everything, absolutely everything, is reason to give him thanks and praise!

A relationship based on love for who I am and grace in spite of what I do causes me to melt in gratitude, humility, and tenderness. When I know that God looks beyond my performance to the woman he loves, I can't but sink into his embrace, recognizing yet again that it is this for which I thirst.

Marilyn Meberg

Refreshed for Service

In 1 Kings 19, after Elijah's victory at Mount Carmel, Jezebel warned that she would have him killed. Terrified, Elijah fled for his life. Finally he sat under a broom tree. Filled with self-pity, he prayed, "I have had enough.... Take my life." He was physically and emotionally exhausted. He continued on his way until he came to a cave, where he retreated. It became a cave of self-pity with an invisible sign over it: Out of Service.

God didn't rebuke or scold him. He loved him just as he was and where he was. But Elijah had his eyes on Jezebel, his circumstances and himself instead of the Lord. He needed a fresh revelation of the Lord. God sent the wind, the earthquake and the fire. Finally Elijah heard the still, small voice. It was God's voice of gentle stillness, a whisper of love for Elijah.

Are you in a cave of disappointment? Failure? Heartache? Have you said, "I'm through"? God cannot use you hidden in a cave. Listen to him lovingly speaking to you in the gentle whisper of the Word. As you listen, you too are cleansed, refreshed and ready for service.

Millie Stamm

A Hair Conditioned Microwave

On one of those days when there are more errands than hours, I decided my hair needed refreshing before stepping outside. Hastily assembling my shampoo supplies, I bustled to the kitchen sink. All went well until it was time to condition. The bottle was tiny, and its cap—the screw-off kind—was smaller still. My hands were wet. But ... with ... determination ... and ... my ... teeth ... whew! I got the lid off and set the bottle back on the counter. Or, at least I thought I did!

In my haste I had actually dropped the conditioner into the sink. I grabbed for the pesky bottle, but it slipped out of my wet hands, this time flopping onto the counter and spraying its contents onto my dry towel.

By now my hands and the bottle were coated with slick, slimy hair conditioner. But I wouldn't quit. I snatched at the bottle again, managing to squeeze its contents onto the microwave across the room!

I knew what I had to do. The last option in the battle of the bottle. I snatched the slimy thing from the counter with my teeth and dropped it in the trash!

The whole battle had taken mere seconds, but the kitchen was in total disarray, and my mouth tasted nothing like "rain"—white or otherwise. What a mess!

As I began to wipe down the walls, floor, counters, appliances, and assembled dishes and flatware that had been hit by the hair conditioner, I realized that my disobedience to God's ways can start with something small like my small conditioner bottle— an unkind word, a rude gesture, a bad attitude—but can easily spread to many areas of my life. As I wiped away each dot of slimy, slippery conditioner, I prayed: "Wash me, too, Lord, and make me clean." With a clean head of hair (and a clean heart, too!) I walked out into a busy Wednesday.

Sarah Hupp

From Betrayal to Blessing

Tamar was the wife of Er, the eldest son of Judah, one of the founders of the twelve tribes of Israel. But Er was a wicked man, who died for his sins. In keeping with the custom of the day, Judah's second son married Tamar so that an heir could be provided for the eldest son. But he, too, behaved wickedly and died.

Already Judah had lost two sons, but he promised Tamar his youngest and only remaining son, instructing her to return to her father's house until the boy was of marriageable age. But the years passed and still there was no marriage.

One day, after Judah's wife died, he set out to shear his sheep. Hearing the news of his journey, Tamar sat down beside the road, disguising herself as a shrine prostitute. That day Judah slept with her, leaving behind his personal seal, cord and staff in pledge of future payment.

About three months later, Judah learned of Tamar's pregnancy. Outraged, he ordered her burned to death. But Tamar sent him a stunning message: "It is by the man to whom these things belong that I am with child."

The man who so quickly passed judgment, little heeding his own tryst with a prostitute, was suddenly taken up short. To his credit, he said, "She is more righteous than I am, since I did not give her to my son." Tamar gave birth to twins.

Distasteful as the story is, God used Tamar's determination to ensure that the tribe of Judah would not only survive but would one day bear the world's Messiah. From Judah's line would come King David and finally, hundreds of years later, Jesus Christ.

Genesis 38 reveals that Tamar was totally unaware of the power of God at work in the events of her life. But he was at work nevertheless, bringing good out of tragedy and blessing out of less than honorable events. And God's power to bring positive things from the negative, even sinful, events of our lives is just as much at work now as in Tamar's day. We may not see it today or tomorrow—or perhaps ever—but we can trust the God we love to do what he loves: bring blessing to us in spite of ourselves.

Jean Syswerda and Ann Spangler

Though I have fallen, I will rise.
Though I sit in darkness,
the LORD will be my light.

MICAH 7:8

Prayer at the End of a Messed-Up Day

Take this day, my Father,
This creased and wrinkled day,
This weary, messed-up day,
Its ragged corners cut me yet,
Still I worry and I fret!
Father, please do not forget
That I am tired
Of this day

Breathe your pure breath, watching Father
On this marred day of mine
This tangled-up day of mine!
Wash it white of stain and spot!
Please cleanse its every blot!
All my mistakes, please remember not
Please fix this day of mine!

BASED ON A POEM BY
ELIZABETH STUART PHELPS

Christ died for us to bring us hope and forgiveness. Peace and joy. Release from the pain of the past—to set our hearts at rest whenever our hearts condemn us. And when we embrace his love and in turn extend it to others, we amazingly find ourselves living a happier life.

Corrie ten Boom described what God does with our mistakes. "He is the greatest artist, but we must surrender. Surrender your blunders to the Lord. He can use them to make the pattern of your life more beautiful."

Chonda Pierce

*Do not be anxious about anything, but in everything, by prayer
and petition, with thanksgiving, present your requests to God.
And the peace of God, which transcends all understanding,
will guard your hearts and your minds in Christ Jesus.*

PHILIPPIANS 4:6–7

Be still, and know that I am God.

PSALM 46:10

*The LORD gives strength to his people;
the LORD blesses his people with peace.*

PSALM 29:11

Jesus loves you passionately, tenaciously, unconditionally. He doesn't depend on e-mail or the telephone to communicate with you. He is never out of the country when you call. He is closer than the air you breathe. If you are running from God because of your past or present lifestyle, he invites you to let him give you peace and rest. He will never leave you or forsake you, because his perfect love is fearless. There is nowhere he's afraid to go, no part of you he's afraid to face.

God pursues those he loves to the ends of the earth. Will you let him find you?

Thelma Wells

God's Beauty Plan

Have you ever noticed how so many of our human loves are more or less conditional? We practice conditional Christmas card sending, keeping lists of who sent Christmas cards last year, so we know whom to include this year. We keep track of who entertained us and to whom we need to reciprocate. We withdraw from relationships that wound us, even if unintentionally. We edit people out of our lives who are too needy or time-consuming. We practice boundaries and measure out love in tiny teaspoons based on merit or loveliness or return on investment.

God's love simplifies all our relational dilemmas. The answer to the people who perplex us is love. God's love, expressed in us, makes us generous of heart. God's love in us transforms our character, enabling us to love a world of lovely and unlovely others. God's love, in us, makes us consistent in character, as kind to the unlovely as to those to whom we are naturally attracted. When we love this way, our souls develop beautifully, connected deeply to both God and to other people. Love is the soul's greatest beautifier!

Valerie Bell

If you are feeling slammed, crushed, broken, undone, unraveled, ripped beyond the point of human endurance ... remember that God's mark on you is bold and sure. You may be "damaged goods," but you are *deliverable*. Straight into his open arms. You *will* reach your final destination and be ushered into the presence of the Lord who is eagerly waiting to claim you as his own, once and for all. There is no unclaimed freight in God's kingdom.

Barbara Johnson

This is what the LORD says ...
"Fear not, for I have redeemed you;
I have summoned you by name; you are mine."
ISAIAH 43:1

Because we live in a fallen world, we will experience negatives in our lives. Heartache and disappointment will come our way. We experience "stuff" we don't deserve, don't want, and can't send back. It's ours. But thanks be to God, nothing happens in this world that he doesn't know about and that he can't handle.

Thelma Wells

The LORD is close to the brokenhearted
and saves those who are crushed in spirit.
PSALM 34:18

God will honor our right attitude. Sometimes he allows difficulties to get our attention and cause us to focus on other areas in our lives that need to be dealt with. Even then, we can pray and boldly beseech the Lord for deliverance. He is a just God who has promised to maintain the cause of the oppressed.

Lisa Fort

God sets us free from everything that would hold us to the earth so we can defy the bonds of the law and soar in freedom with him. Why don't Christians race to this truth, embrace it, and live the rest of their lives in freedom instead of in bondage? I believe it's because they don't trust themselves with grace. It seems too free, without strict guidelines. They don't quite know what to do without a bunch of rules that tell them exactly how to behave. I mean, what if they make a mistake? It's just too outrageous to them to think that God would trust them with this much freedom. But he does.

Luci Swindoll

The Lord does not treat us as our sins deserve

or repay us according to our iniquities.

For as high as the heavens are above the earth,

so great is his love for those who fear him;

as far as the east is from the west,

so far has he removed our transgressions from us.

PSALM 103:10–12

If anyone is in Christ, he is a new creation;

the old has gone, the new has come!

2 CORINTHIANS 5:17

I will be their God,

and they will be my people.

No longer will a man teach his neighbor,

or a man his brother, saying, "Know the Lord,"

because they will all know me,

from the least of them to the greatest.

For I will forgive their wickedness

and will remember their sins no more.

HEBREWS 8:10–12

There's Safety in God's Plan

A man was obliged to descend into a deep well by sliding down a fixed rope which was supposed to be of ample length. But to his dismay he came to the end of it before his feet had touched the bottom. He had not the strength to climb up again, and to let go and drop might mean he would be dashed to pieces in the depths below. He held on until his strength was utterly exhausted, and then he dropped, as he thought, to his death. He fell—just three inches—and found himself safe on the rock bottom.

Are you afraid to take this step? Does it seem too sudden, too much like a leap in the dark? Do you not know that the step of faith always "falls on the seeming void, but finds the rock beneath"? If ever you are to enter God's glorious land, flowing with milk and honey, you must sooner or later step into the brimming waters, for there is no other path; and to do it now may save you months and even years of disappointment and grief.

Hannah Whitall Smith

The Big Picture

Sue, a devoted parent-volunteer, used the PTA's new popcorn machine to treat her son's fourth-grade class to a popcorn party. Unfortunately, when she set up the popper, she unknowingly parked it right under a heat sensor. Fifteen minutes later the popcorn started popping, the fire alarms went off, and the whole school evacuated.

And did I mention it was November? And raining cats and dogs?

When the principal came galloping down the hallway, he pointed to the heat sensor flashing above the popcorn popper and yelled, "Do you know what you've done?" Sue was sure those students and their teachers would never forgive her for sending them out into a driving rainstorm.

A few days later the principal called. "Quit focusing on this one incident and look at the big picture," he said. "I forgive you—and the kids thought it was great. They love getting out of class, even if it means standing out in the rain."

The next week, Sue opened the school's storeroom where the popcorn cart was parked. It took a moment to realize why it looked different. On top, someone had added a flashing red light. And hanging from one of the cart's handles was a little firefighter's helmet with her name hand-lettered on the front. She looked at that popcorn cart and did something she wouldn't have believed a few days earlier. She laughed.

When we have hope, we can look at the big picture rather than focus on our mistakes. No matter what happens to us—or what havoc we unintentionally wreak on others—we will be able to learn from our mistakes and start over. We'll even be able to do what we never thought we could do: laugh again.

Barbara Johnson

FEELING OUT OF CONTROL?
GOD'S IN CONTROL!

Coincidence ... Or God's Plan?

I'm amazed at the number of situations that seem to be coincidences—until I stop to take a look at the whole picture. For instance, I never thought of myself as an author until a set of circumstances started the pages to roll off the presses.

One of my business associates, without my knowledge, recommended me as a speaker for a national organization. I found out about it when the conference coordinator called to tell me I had been selected. When the time neared that I was to speak, the organization called my office and asked that my books be at the conference by a certain date.

"My books? Did she say, 'My books'?" I spouted to anyone who was within hearing. "I don't have *one* book, let alone *books*. Nobody told me you were supposed to be published to speak for this group. They want 'my books' in six weeks!"

My daughter Vikki was in the office at the time and immediately took the telephone from me. She wrote down the instructions on where the books should be delivered, agreed that I would have a book there on or before the date, hung up the phone, and handed me one of the greatest challenges of my life. "Write the book!" she said. "You know you have all the information you need. It's time to stop procrastinating and do it. You'll write on the plane, in your hotel room, everywhere you can. Send the information back to me and don't worry about the rest. You will have a book at the conference. You can do it; I know you can! Now get on it!"

With Vikki's tenacity, my knowledge and determination, the help of other people who assisted on the project, and God's grace, the book was delivered by the required date. But this was no coincidence. God had placed the material for the book in my mind and heart several years before; the speaking engagement just prodded me to do the writing. God had lined up all the circumstances to make it happen.

I was fifty-two years old when I wrote my first book. Now, at fifty-seven, I have either written or coauthored six books. This writing frenzy all started with a friend suggesting me as a speaker for a conference. And the "coincidences" go on.

I was standing in line with two friends to board an airplane to Salt Lake City when a lady and her daughter noticed my purple and white Women of Faith tote bag. The mother asked if we had attended a conference, adding that they had been to one in Lakeland, Florida, the previous year.

"We've been trying to contact one of the speakers," she said. Then she looked at me and said, "The bee! The bee! You're the one! You're the one with the bumblebee pins! You're the one we've been trying to locate for more than three weeks!"

As you look back over the circumstances of your life, can you discern the carefully planned patterns that at first looked like coincidence? Situations don't always follow our plans, but God orchestrates our lives nonetheless.

Thelma Wells

The plans of the LORD stand firm forever,
  the purposes of his heart through all generations.
  PSALM 33:11

Many are the plans in a man's heart,
  but it is the LORD's purpose that prevails.
  PROVERBS 19:21

May God give you the desire of your heart
  and make all your plans succeed.
  PSALM 20:4

For Such a Time as This

Esther never really wanted to be a wife of the king. But God's plan for Esther included this unusual circumstance. When Esther's uncle Mordecai asked her to intercede with the king for the Jews' deliverance, Mordecai reminded her that she might have been placed in "royal position for such a time as this" (Esther 4:14).

Esther had a choice. She could have chosen to stand aside and let someone else be Israel's spokesperson. But because of her faith, Esther chose to follow God's plan, and her courage and obedience have been celebrated for centuries.

God has a plan for your life, too, the way he wants things to be. His plan may mean some difficult choices, some fearsome paths, some uncertain outcomes. But you do have a choice: You can choose to follow the crowd or courageously yield to the Creator.

Sarah Hupp

A Double Blessing

Trust is such a lovely word in a world thoroughly self-indulged and complicated. It is quiet. Simple. It represents freedom. Letting go.

A couple, who had been down the battered road of infertility, longed for a baby. A perfect situation came about. A young birth mother who felt the only answer for her baby was adoption.

A precious baby girl was born. The adoptive couple came from another city to meet the birth mother to take their new baby home. The birth mother signed the papers, releasing the baby from the hospital. But in the courtroom, days later, she broke down. She just couldn't give up her baby.

The couple's celebration turned to heartbreak. Immediately, they began to trust. They waited quietly. In a year, twin girls were born and theirs was the chosen family. They lost one, and God gave them back two.

There are very many unknowns in life. A husband's job. Our children's struggles. A tentative move. Bills to pay. Aged parents to look after.

Let go completely. Trust. Live with it all in an open hand before God. Jesus promises he *will* work it *all* out.

Ann Kiemel Anderson

The Lord of Change

Not all change is by choice. A marriage dissolves. Cherished friendships change in character or another person's choice cuts directly across our own, bringing us where we never wanted to be. A career change, voluntary or involuntary, may disrupt our lives. Financial losses sweep away our props. Even geographic change can be disorienting.

For the believer, then, the question is vital: Is our God the Lord of change? Will he be with us in change, especially when it strains our trust to its limit? Ironically, while we trust him with our eternal fate, we may find it difficult to trust him for next month's car payment, a new relationship, or an unexpected turn in our lives.

In the kaleidoscopic whirl of our life patterns, it can be enormously reassuring to remind ourselves that God is unchanging: "I the LORD do not change" (Malachi 3:6).

Gini Andrews

Do not look forward in fear to the changes of life;
Rather look to them with full hope that as they arise,
God, whose very own you are, will lead you safely through
all things;
And when you cannot stand it, God will carry you in His arms.
Do not fear what may happen tomorrow;
The same everlasting Father who cares for you today
will take care of you today and every day.

ST. FRANCIS DE SALES

Someone to Trust

At one time, my soul was marked by anxiety and shattered trust concerning God's intentions for my future. My forty-year-old soul was afraid of life. The soul of today points 180 degrees in the opposite direction. This soul embraces life.

Shortly after my cancer diagnosis, God reassured me that my life was not out of control. "Valerie, you will live as long as intended by my will. Not a day more. Not a day less." What a relief. It was as if my soul let out a deep sigh and then relaxed. I did not need to feel any responsibility about the timing of my body wearing out. God was in charge. I was in his perfect will. I could trust God with my life one day at a time.

Valerie Bell

Strength When You Need It

My mother died of cancer. She showed amazing courage throughout her illness and handled the dying process with dignity and humility. She was prodded, poked, operated on, and carted back and forth to hospitals, but she never once complained, only confessed that she was "getting tired." Before my eyes she lived out the truth: "God will give you strength when you need it."

Of all the words my mother spoke, I think that statement has meant the most. When I was in the middle of the most difficult times of my life—the struggles, the tears, the dark days—she would offer those tender words. Now, as I look back and see that God really was with me, giving me grace to bear the unbearable, I realize that my mother was right. More than that, I know she spoke the heart of God.

There is no situation in this life that he will not miraculously lead us through—giving us a strength and peace that we know is beyond anything we could conjure up. Lean on him. Abandon yourself to his grace. God will give you strength when you need it.

Kathy Troccoli

Those who know your name will trust in you,
for you, LORD, have never forsaken those who seek you.
PSALM 9:10

Those who trust in the LORD are like Mount Zion,
which cannot be shaken but endures forever.
PSALM 125:1

The LORD longs to be gracious to you;
he rises to show you compassion.
For the LORD is a God of justice.
Blessed are all who wait for him!
ISAIAH 30:18

"Sim"-ple Destiny

Computer simulation games have found their way into my house. My children and grandchildren enjoy the sensation of mastering railroads and roller coasters, cities and civilizations, towers and tribes. With a basic understanding of the rules and a few, deft keystrokes, a participant can control the destinies and comfort of nameless thousands—and become wealthy tycoons in the process.

How grateful I am that God doesn't treat his relationship with his children like a computer simulation game. I am not a nameless face in the crowd to him, nor just a means for him to make a name for himself. The Bible reassures me that I am God's child (Romans 8:16), that he delights over me (Zephaniah 3:17), that he has chosen a special name for me when I reach heaven (Revelation 2:17), and that his plans for my destiny are always for my good (Jeremiah 29:11). No "sim"-ple plans for me, thank you. I'll take what God has in store instead!

Sarah Hupp

Trust that whatever action God is taking—or not taking—
in your life right now is for your highest good. God knows what
he's doing.

Marilyn Meberg

I would rather walk with God in the dark than go alone in
the light.

Mary Gardiner Brainard

What do you do when a storm hits? What stabilizes your life?
Our stabilizers are: I am *his!* I believe *him!* I serve *him!* Nothing
can move us, for our anchor in Jesus Christ stabilizes our lives.

Millie Stamm

No matter what comes into our day, we should relinquish our desire to strike back, to vindicate, to look good, to shame another, to let anger take hold, to have our own way. I get so bogged down in the frustrating specifics of life that I lose sight of the goal of life: *to become more like Christ.* When I let go and trust that God is totally in control, I can fly—even with broken wings. How happy it must make God when one of his children lives and loves with this level of understanding and grace.

Sheila Walsh

Sometimes I choose to hang on to the impending doom of the moment or I try to rush the punch line. My mother, on the other hand, has chosen to simply relax, hold on to her purse, and smile at the flowers in the fields. She is content and willing to wait upon God's timing. Will she never stop teaching me? Probably not!

Chonda Pierce

The Shunammite woman of 2 Kings 4 knew there was hope even in the most devastating of circumstances, even though her little son lay dead on Elisha's couch. "It's all right," she said to her husband, knowing full well that their boy was gone. She knew God wouldn't forsake her.

"It's all right." Can you express that sentiment even when it seems like your world is crashing in on you? Even in the most agonizing of circumstances, even when you feel abandoned, even when tragedy strikes—he's there. Trust his word and gain assurance from the Shunammite woman who, in the midst of appalling circumstances, could say, "It's all right."

Jean Syswerda and Ann Spangler

Oswald Chambers once wrote, "Faith never knows where it is being led, but it loves and knows the One who is leading." That's my prayer: to know the One who *is* in control. To trust him. To love him.

Sheila Walsh

Nothing this side of heaven is absolute. Nothing is forever. Hair will be shorn; hair will grow back (usually). Faces will fall, no matter how many times we get them lifted. My losses can't be recouped. The future is unknown. Times change, we change, everything changes.

Another bottom-line truth comes to mind: "I the Lord do not change" (Malachi 3:6). Whew! Nothing remains the same ... *except God.* God's character is immutable and his Word is final. His stubborn love for us never varies or wavers. Regardless of our behavior, our losses, the length of our hair, or the droop of our face, God's promises are true, and his love holds us fast.

Barbara Johnson

Laughter Is Loving

Our God loves to hear his children loving him. When we are seeking after the joy of his heart—then we laugh. We laugh in the right place, at the right time. God's perfect timing! To me, God's grace is that incredible element in our lives that allows us to somehow pass through devastation, poverty, embarrassment, heartache, or grief and somehow—in his time—stand on the other side grinning, because his "grace is sufficient" (2 Corinthians 12:9).

I've seen joy return again and again. I've watched the tears— but I've also heard the laughter . . . the laughs of those who have suffered the loss of home, the pain of abuse, the anguish of divorce, the loneliness of rejection, and even the loss of a child. They are testaments that his grace is indeed sufficient, and they have found joy and laughter once again—sometimes after believing it was gone forever.

Laughter is the indication that life will go on—the darkness will pass. God's sweet hands of mercy and grace brush away fears and "rejoicing comes in the morning" (Psalm 30:5).

Chonda Pierce

Today we may be facing problems and situations that have no visible solution. We may be looking at our problems with our physical eyes. We may be crying out, "What shall we do?" When our eyes are on our circumstances we panic. When they are on God we are at rest. By faith our inner eyes can see God's provision for us. We may not see our way out of our problem, but we can trust God to encircle us in the midst of it.

Millie Stamm

I will not doubt, though all my ships at sea
Come drifting home with broken masts and sails;
I shall believe the hand which never fails,
From seeming evil worketh good to me.
And, though I weep because those sails are battered,
Still will I cry, while my best hopes lie shattered,
"I trust in thee."

ELLA WHEELER WILCOX

I know God will not give me anything I can't handle. I just wish he didn't trust me so much.

Mother Teresa

When things go well it is possible to live on the surface for years; but when sorrow comes, such as that experienced when a loved one dies, one has to go deep into the things of life. It is there that we find solace and new strength. It is there that through the comfort and compassion of God, beauty enters the soul.

Jean Jackson-Swopes

John 14:27 says, "Peace I leave with you; my peace I give you. I do not give to you as the world gives. Do not let your hearts be troubled and do not be afraid." What a wonderful promise and consolation in a world that measures us according to the level of our prowess instead of according to our virtue and service. Stand firm, women of God, and having done everything, continue to stand (Ephesians 6:13).

Carolyn Parks

May the God of peace, who through the blood of the eternal covenant brought back from the dead our Lord Jesus, that great Shepherd of the sheep, equip you with everything good for doing his will, and may he work in us what is pleasing to him, through Jesus Christ, to whom be glory for ever and ever. Amen.

HEBREWS 13:20–21

The book of Genesis reveals how hard it was for Sarah to remember God's promises and to wait for him to fulfill them in his timing, which is often on a calendar far different from our own.

Waiting patiently for God to work may be one of the most difficult experiences of our Christian walk. We live in an age of the immediate. We think waiting, and doing so *quietly*, is somehow less worthy, perhaps even a bit lazy. Whatever the circumstances, God's timing is the best timing. When you're tempted to step in and make things happen on your own, think of Sarah. Her attempts to fulfill God's promise of a son through her servant Hagar had disastrous results. Remember that God has his own timetable, and rest in the assurance that he loves you and will fulfill his promises to you.

Jean Syswerda and Ann Spangler

God's timing is impeccable, as always. His love runs deeper than the circumstances, rejections, hurts, or pains. His Holy Spirit always shows up when we invite him into every moment in our lives. Always right on time at just the right moment.

Chonda Pierce

God knows the way that I take;
when he has tested me, I will come forth as gold.

JOB 23:10

We also rejoice in our sufferings, because we know that
suffering produces perseverance; perseverance, character;
and character, hope. And hope does not disappoint us,
because God has poured out his love into our hearts
by the Holy Spirit, whom he has given us.

ROMANS 5:3–5

Trouble is universal. No one escapes it. But what do we do about it? We can worry, panic, be fearful and feel sorry for ourselves, or we can commit our trouble to the Lord, trusting him to take us through it.

Millie Stamm

When faith is small and hope doubts, love conquers. We never have to live in fear because God's love is perfect.

Thelma Wells

You can spend your whole life grabbing control and never be free—or you can say yes to God without fear, let go into his arms of love, and be set free—finally free ... finally "getting it" that God is good.

Sheila Walsh

Popcorn Wisdom

What is there about time and its relationship to healing?

I remember hearing that phrase "Time will heal things" so often that I decided that I would never pass that word of wisdom on to any broken-hearted mourner sitting on the family couch in a funeral home. But in recent years, when I find myself searching for the right words for someone grieving, that very sentence has slipped off my tongue.

I've said it, and yet I have learned that "time" itself doesn't heal much of anything. *Time* is not what counts; it's what we allow to happen *during* that passage of time. If we put too much stock in the idea that if only time will hurry up and pass, then everything will be all right, we wind up watching the clock—believing the passing seconds are doing something valuable for us, believing that perhaps even some healing is taking place, simply because the clock is ticking—and we wind up burning the popcorn.

My husband does lots of things well, but cooking is not one of them. To his credit, over the years he has taken the trouble to memorize the recipe for microwavable popcorn: put the bag in with THIS SIDE UP facing up, punch three-and-a-half minutes, and serve hot. But not long ago I got a new microwave. My husband took charge of family night by volunteering for popcorn duty. He punched in the time like so many nights before and three-and-a-half minutes later we were opening windows and fanning smoke.

"That time has always worked before!" he cried, using a pillow to fan away the smoke.

"But you didn't check the wattage of the microwave, did you?" I responded.

He shook his head, guilty.

In God's scheme chronological time is not the measure of "fullness" or "ripeness." Think about the popcorn David cooked (burnt). He was assuming that three-and-a-half minutes "on" would do the job right. What he didn't think about was the extra power of this new oven.

So, it's not time alone that cooks (or burns), or ripens, or educates, or heals—it's *what goes on during that time.* How much heat is generated? How much sunshine is present? How many courses do you complete? How will you let God minister to your pain?

Time doesn't heal our spirits. God does—as we give him permission to work in us, through us, and with us. And that healing can start today.

Chonda Pierce

Most of us know what we *don't* want in life, but not so many of us know what we *do* want. And not having what we want, or not wanting what we have, leads to discontentment, if not hopelessness and despair. But I've learned that there are ways around these feelings. We can keep accumulating, trying to find what we *might* want, what's missing. We can learn to pretend that we're completely-satisfied-thank-you. Or ... we can do the one and only thing that works: turn to God and his Word. It is he who brings about real change in our lives ... by giving us hope.

Luci Swindoll

A Constant Companion

With all my years of traveling, I've slept in some strange places. My great comfort when I'm far away from home is that the Lord never sleeps but watches over me whether I'm in Bangkok, Britain, or Boise, Idaho.

I remember staying with an old lady in Bristol, England, who had forty-three cats. I like cats, but forty-three are about forty-two cats too many for me. I drank my cup of cocoa with cat fur in it, and then thanked my hostess and headed to bed.

"My little darlings will follow you!" she sang out after me.

I turned to see a plague of fur flow after me. "That's all right," I said. "I can find my room."

"It's where my darlings sleep, too!" She smiled as she delivered this good news.

Fluffy, Muffy, and the gang made themselves comfortable on the bed, in my suitcase, and in my toilet bag. We were a family.

I woke up to find I was suffocating. I must be in a cave, a tunnel, I was drowning ... no, it was worse than that. "Help, Lord, there's a cat on my face!"

I have lots of fun stories to tell and laugh about. But every story is held together by the common thread of God's faithfulness through it all. He was my constant companion.

Is it ever hard for you to close your eyes at night? Do you worry about what tomorrow will hold or if you will be safe until morning? Psalm 121 makes it clear God never closes his eyes. He is always watching over you ... even if you have fur in your mouth.

Sheila Walsh

If your every human plan and calculation has miscarried, if, one by one, human props have been knocked out, and doors have shut in your face, take heart. God is trying to get a message through to you, and the message is: "Stop depending on inadequate human resources. Let me handle the matter."

Catherine Wood Marshall

When a sweet and gentle spirit can breeze across sunken shoulders and whisper peace and joy to broken hearts—that's when you must throw up your hands and say, "There is no explanation. It is undeniably God, and in him there is joy and laughter after the rain. After the pain."

Chonda Pierce

Our outlandish, fearless, stubborn God watches over every single one of us. With tender parental attention. With perfect sovereign intention. That's just the kind of dad he is.

Sheila Walsh

The LORD is good to those whose hope is in him,
  to the one who seeks him.

LAMENTATIONS 3:25

God who watches over you will not slumber;
  indeed, he who watches over Israel
  will neither slumber nor sleep.
The LORD watches over you—
  the LORD is your shade at your right hand;
the sun will not harm you by day,
  nor the moon by night.

PSALM 121:3–6

Laugh at the Days to Come

I look to an extraordinary woman for help as I approach the unfamiliar future. She has no name. She is known simply as the Proverbs 31 woman.

I challenge you to examine more closely one of her lesser-praised characteristics. To me, it is the most amazing thing ever written about any person: "She can laugh at the days to come." Amazing!

Picture this woman. Her gray head is thrown back, lifting toward heaven a deeply wrinkled face. Her belly bulges, her legs are marbled with blue rivulets cresting their banks, and her dimples have long ago disappeared, buried deeply in wrinkles, but somehow she seems incredibly attractive. She "youngs" before your very eyes, her spirit shining through. Even while experiencing deteriorating health and beauty, she laughs. Though frail, she laughs with confidence, with spunk, abandon, and class. She is not afraid of what lies ahead. She embraces "the days to come."

This is the plucky quality I want to achieve in the second half of my life journey. One year closer to the reality of death? Yes. But I have a plan of my own. I intend to have the last laugh!

Valerie Bell

A wife of noble character who can find?
    She is worth far more than rubies.
Her husband has full confidence in her
    and lacks nothing of value.
She brings him good, not harm,
    all the days of her life....
She sets about her work vigorously;
    her arms are strong for her tasks....
She is clothed with strength and dignity;
    she can laugh at the days to come.
She speaks with wisdom,
    and faithful instruction is on her tongue....
Her children arise and call her blessed;
    her husband also, and he praises her:
"Many women do noble things,
    but you surpass them all."
Charm is deceptive, and beauty is fleeting;
    but a woman who fears the LORD is to be praised.

PROVERBS 31:10–12, 17, 25–26, 28–30

NOBODY'S PERFECT (WHEW!)

Righteous in Him!

I have no trouble believing that God is who he says he is, and that I'm his child because of his great plan. I have no trouble at all being sure about God; it's me I can't be sure of. Some days I can't be sure of anything. Some days, even though I feel *very* sure and self-confident, I end up falling on my face.

My face turns red just thinking about the time I lost my slip when introduced at a prestigious banquet, or another time when my jacket fell open at a business meeting revealing my Victoria's secrets, or the time I wore two totally different shoes—shoes that didn't resemble each other in any way!

Then there are the times I think I'm a "perfect me" Christian and I fail. Oh, how I fail! My imperfections (and you have no idea how many there are) remind me that he is perfect, he is righteous, and that even though I don't deserve it, *I am made righteous in him!*

Sue Buchanan

A Plan for Your Soul

The college-aged pizza delivery boy had called me "ma'am." It jarred me. I know what "ma'am" means. Young men do not call cute young chickies "ma'am." It is a euphemism they politely hide behind when they think you are not really a living breathing woman but a fossilized specimen from the antediluvian period. They say "ma'am"; they mean "old relic."

I could no longer live in denial. My body was failing me on several levels. The eventual benefits of working out, the swallowing of antioxidants, slathering of alpha hydroxyl creams, low-fat dieting, sweating, pumping, and sliding, and the spending of big bucks can be summed up succinctly: We might look younger than the next person, but we will all eventually experience that blessing while wearing a coffin.

Growing older really should not bother us at all. Whether our birthday cakes glow sweetly with sixteen candles or blaze with a bonfire of eighty-eight, we are all in the "I'm losing it" process.

But there is good news. We are body *and soul.* We were created to operate with two realities: inner—spiritual, and outer—physical, including our appearance and health. It is a gift to know that truth. Even though it is sad that our bodies are temporary, the upside is the understanding that we are so much more than body.

Learning to care for my soul was what healed my wounded self. No bodywork, be it cosmetic or health-oriented, can heal the soul in an aging woman's life. Tend the body, but be realistic enough to admit that your body will never be as good at seventy as it was at seventeen.

Grieve if you must, but be aware of an emerging wonderful reality—new possibilities and potentials are opening to you. Care for your soul and you can be better at seventy than you were at seventeen. Care for your soul and you have made an enormous stride toward quality living. Care for your soul and experience confidence, joy, and inner strength.

Valerie Bell

*You do not lack any spiritual gift as you eagerly wait for our Lord
Jesus Christ to be revealed. He will keep you strong to the end,
so that you will be blameless on the day of our Lord Jesus Christ.*
1 CORINTHIANS 1:7–8

*Every good and perfect gift is from above, coming
down from the Father of the heavenly lights, who
does not change like shifting shadows.*
JAMES 1:17

God's gifts put man's best dreams to shame.
ELIZABETH BARRETT BROWNING

Art Appreciation

When you began to put together
The days of my life
You must have known
Where each piece would go ...
You've told me that I am
Fearfully and wonderfully
Made ...
And I believe you, Lord,
I do!
I may not be a velvet tapestry,
But even crazy-quilts
Have purpose,
To give warmth and
Cozy comfort and
Color to a room!
Whatever I am, Lord,
You made me ...
Lovingly,
Carefully,
Reverently,
And exactly right!

JOY MORGAN DAVIS

The Ordinary Body of Christ

I often talk to people who tell me they are ordinary, that they have nothing to offer and couldn't possibly be used by God. I tell them, "The Gaithers were school teachers in Indiana. That's pretty ordinary!" Gloria thought she was a failure because she didn't get to realize her dreams either to go to the mission field or become a second Barbara Walters. Yet God used her in a totally unexpected way as a lyricist, author, speaker, and as cohost of the Gaither Homecoming videos.

No one is ordinary in God's sight! It strikes me that God can use plain ol' simple Spam and baloney eaters as his servants every bit as well as he can use big ol' brainy theologians with their discussions about Darwin. I'm amazed at the people God chooses to help build up the body of Christ. A pretty weird bunch! I'm in awe of the fact that I'm one of them. And so are you!

Sue Buchanan

Not *That* Gift!

Sometimes God gives us gifts that are hard for us to enjoy or appreciate so we misuse them. He graces us with a day of rest apart from the turmoil, but instead of enjoying his soothing presence we fill the quiet with television or mindless activity. He sends a friend to support us when we're blue, but because it isn't exactly who we want to be with we brush her off and miss the gift. He gives us an opportunity to forgive, but we cling to our bitterness and hold on to the grudge. He offers us a chance to be taught something new, but we're too proud to learn. The list goes on.

We need to recognize how often we mistrust the Lord and reject his gracious gifts because they're not on our terms. Then we can tell him how disappointed we are. He meets us in our honesty, mends us with his grace, and pours the oil of his love all over us. Even if things are still not in perfect alignment, we're able to move forward.

Luci Swindoll

> *As a father has compassion on his children,*
> *so the LORD has compassion on those who fear him;*
> *for he knows how we are formed,*
> *he remembers that we are dust.*
>
> PSALM 103:13–14

I'm not sure if my humanity or my insecurity is responsible, but I'm given to the misconception that, when I slip and mess up, I must earn my way back into God's good graces. I'm grateful I'm not God. His heart, unlike mine, isn't narrow. Only his path is.

Patsy Clairmont

We waste so much time nursing regrets over lost jobs or soured relationships; we harbor shame for things poorly done. But dwelling on what cannot be changed will only steal our precious joy today. When things go slow, go bad, go sour, or go away, it's time to unwrap the life preserver of God's love and stay afloat on the boundless ocean of his grace.

Barbara Johnson

Go With God

The story of Jesus in the temple can teach us something about our own relationship with God. Mary and Joseph had made their plans to return to Nazareth. They set off early in the morning with their family and traveled for a whole day without Jesus, assuming he was with them. Sometimes, I think we tend to do the same thing. We make our plans, tell God what we intend to do, and then travel for quite a while before we realize that he simply isn't with us! It isn't that he leaves us on purpose because he wants to embarrass us or show us who's really the boss. It's just that in the rush and hurry to get something done, we may ride roughshod over love, humility or what we know to be God's will for us, and we leave him far, far behind, lost in the crowd.

If we try to go ahead of God's enabling power, then we, like Joseph and Mary, will have to retrace our steps. Certainly the goal may lie clearly ahead. It may be purely spiritual, or it may be a more immediate piece of practical work. In either case, we can't go at it any faster than God wants us to. We have to wait and learn the lessons on the road. If God will not go ahead with us, we must wait and go with God.

Marcia Hollis

Growing God's Way

When our children were born, my husband and I lovingly cared for them daily. We held them close, rocked them to sleep and fed them. As they were able, we encouraged them to learn to walk, dress themselves and communicate. We watched excitedly as they grew.

Likewise, our heavenly Father is actively involved in our growth; he encourages us according to our capabilities and understanding at the time. He does not push us; he waits until we are ready. If God told us everything about ourselves and life all at once, we would be confused and crushed. Instead he teaches us based on our spiritual and emotional age level. God's gentle unfolding plan increases our insight and encourages our consistent growth.

Joan C. Webb

Manual Labor

My spiffy new jalopy was parked in the driveway just waiting for me. I had driven the vehicle only a couple times, so, when a frosty Sunday morning rolled around, I headed out to drive my darling to church. After finally figuring out how to adjust my seat and strap on my seat belt, I tackled the defroster.

I couldn't find the right button. I did locate the sunroof button. About a quarter inch of fresh snow accumulated on my hairdo before I re-found the sunroof button and shut the thing.

From the glove compartment I fished out the owner's manual. Printed across the book's cover in large letters was this message: "Read Manual Before Operating Vehicle." (Groan.)

That's the bottom line, folks: if we don't know how to operate what we have, it will be of little value to us. The same is true of understanding God's workings. If we're not intimately familiar with his manual, what are the chances we'll understand his ways?

Patsy Clairmont

Do you remember in Numbers 22, when God spoke to Balaam through the mouth of Balaam's donkey? Balaam had been instructed by God to give a specific message to the king of the Moabites. Balaam took a little license with what he knew to be God's message, so God opened the donkey's mouth, and a two-way conversation began between Balaam and his mule. As a result, Balaam realized God was displeased with him. Confessing his disobedience, Balaam promised to say the very words God had spoken. The donkey shut up when Balaam shaped up.

Marilyn Meberg

I have a feeling that laughter in a "no laughing zone" has been going on for a long, long time. There had to be incidents when God must have watched his creation unfold and sometimes just sat back and grinned, even chuckled out loud. When did Adam find out that bees sting? Better yet, *how* did Adam find out that bees sting? How did Eve learn that a cactus does not make for a very good seat cushion? You know God must have had some great laughs!

Chonda Pierce

Patchwork Confessions

Amish women have long been regarded as quilt masters. Their works command high prices because of the intricacy of stitching superimposed over very simple colors and patterns. Yet every Amish quilt carries a spiritual message, too. Recognizing that only God is perfect, every Amish quilt contains an error, a visual reminder that though human beings may grow and learn and do many things well, they will never be perfect. As the Amish quilter places the errored block in her quilt she asks forgiveness for her imperfections, trusting a perfect, loving God to hear and answer.

Many times I have been tempted to strut like a peacock in my pride of perfectionism. But now a quilt hangs on my wall as a visible reminder that nobody's perfect. Nobody but God.

Sarah Hupp

An Embarrassed Masterpiece

Not long after I had breast cancer surgery and was still feeling very body-conscious, I had an important client meeting. It not only included several representatives from the company I was producing for, but several equipment suppliers as well. I wasn't just on the spot to come up with workable ideas, but I was in charge of leading the meeting and responsible to negotiate a win-win situation for everyone.

That morning I dressed carefully. I put on my new electric-blue pantsuit that Wayne had bought me in Chicago—my *very fashionable, and in my opinion, quite stunning electric-blue pantsuit —* the drama of which was in the draping effect of the neckline. You could wear it without a blouse and pull the draping to one shoulder and attach it to a large, asymmetrical button.

The meeting went well at first, but somewhere along the way the negotiations with one of the vendors broke down. We simply couldn't come to an agreement. At last, in frustration, I stood to my feet, smacked the table with my palm, put my hands on my hips, and said, "I'm sorry. This just isn't working for me."

Wow! Everyone came to attention like a precision drill team; shoulders straightened, chins dropped, and mouths flew open. Just as I was mentally patting myself on the back for being so savvy in my leadership skills, all eyes shifted from my face to my chest. My eyes followed their gaze. One whole side of me—albeit covered in a black lace bra and draped in electric blue—had popped out for the world to see!

The room got so quiet you could have heard an ant breathing. Finally, one of the men broke the silence. He turned to the others and said, "Well, it sure is working for me."

In Ephesians 2:10 it says that "we are God's workmanship." Another translation uses the word "masterpiece." I certainly wasn't thinking about being God's masterpiece that memorable day. I laughed with the others, but I must say I was more than slightly embarrassed.

But think about it! I'm a masterpiece! You're a masterpiece! Isn't that another reason for us to be lavish with our praise? You are God's child; you are beautiful; you are talented; you are a true gift to life!

Sue Buchanan

In Everything Give Thanks

God's definition of thankfulness and mine are often a universe apart. God says we should give thanks in everything. I struggle with that. I think he could not mean that literally. I want to give thanks for the things that bring me joy and cause me happiness. When we thank God for sorrowful intruders, frustrating circumstances, or maddening relationships, we are indicating to God that we trust him to work out in our lives that which is best for us.

Thankfulness is not a child's verse at the supper table. It's not doll-like pilgrims decorating a festive, autumnal holiday table. The everyday practice of thankfulness is powerful, capable of changing our entire perspective on life. Thankfulness is what keeps our ships from going down when life's seas threaten to swamp us. It also helps us to realize the blessings we experience in the everyday nitty-gritty mundaneness of our lives.

For instance, I'm learning I can thank God for the dust in my home. You see, in my home dust is not just dust. It is the accumulating evidence of my lack of homemaking ability. Some women do not understand this struggle of mine. They are the ones who only have new dust in their homes, the kind that whisks off surfaces with a light swipe or feather duster. I do not have new dust in my home. My dust is old dust. Old dust becomes a part of the molecular structure of the surface it is covering. It becomes ingrained, gritty, sticky, and removable only by sandpaper. It is my accuser.

But I am learning to look at my dust differently these days. A new perspective has taught me that if dust is covering my things, then I *have things*. Refugees do not worry about dust. You and I have dust because we are prosperous, rich even, compared to many. A grateful spirit can transform a house of burden into a home of blessing, a life of sadness into a life of blessing.

Valerie Bell

ALL THINGS WORK TOGETHER
FOR THE GOOD ... REALLY!

Donkey Days

Dear God, I just couldn't help it:
I chuckled aloud this morning as I read the story of Saul—
How one very ordinary day
At the urgent request of his father
Saul combed the hillside searching for lost donkeys.
Little did he know that Samuel waited to anoint him
That very day as Israel's first king.
The story refreshed and delighted me.
Far too often I bewail my daily routine.
My days with their nitty-gritty seem no more challenging than
    hunting for lost donkeys—
Stubborn obstinate donkeys.
But suddenly this morning
There came a flash of fresh insight:
You do indeed have a plan for me.
You have a settled purpose.
I am guided by your wisdom and love.
And all you ask is my confident trust.
Dreary days? Donkey days?
Yes, Lord—often. But just around the corner
Or at the top of a hill
You wait with a shining surprise!

RUTH HARMS CALKIN

So do not fear, for I am with you;
do not be dismayed, for I am your God.
I will strengthen you and help you;
I will uphold you with my righteous right hand.
ISAIAH 41:10

Jesus said: "Surely I am with you always,
to the very end of the age."
MATTHEW 28:20

When you pass through the waters,
I will be with you;
and when you pass through the rivers,
they will not sweep over you.
When you walk through the fire,
you will not be burned;
the flames will not set you ablaze.
For I am the LORD, your God,
the Holy One of Israel, your Savior."
ISAIAH 43:2–3

Puny, Provincial Plans

When I married my husband, I sorrowfully abandoned my dreams, one by one. Because of his calling to the ministry, I believed we would be church-mouse poor, and I would never see the world. I would lead a provincial and boring life!

We have been married for thirty years now and looking back, I am so grateful God intervened in our life's goals. I had planned for security. Fortunately, God planned for growth. Ministry has been rewarding, personally stretching, a backdrop for growth on multiple levels, and surprisingly fulfilling! My plans, in retrospect, are the ones that seemed provincial and boring!

Several years into our marriage and ministry, I tasted the irony of my puny plans and God's intervention as I drank in the experience of being in Machu Picchu, the Lost City of the Incas, leading a student missionary trip that brought us to the Andes Mountains of Peru. What a great experience to serve these children of God, to participate in their lives, to worship together, if only for a brief time. I never could have anticipated during my college years that missions would fascinate me in the least. It occurred to me during that trip all I would have missed if I had settled for a more calculated, secure material plan!

Valerie Bell

Joy comes in the morning. Joanna discovered this in a miraculous way on Jesus' resurrection day. She went to his tomb expecting to minister to his dead body and to grieve. Instead, her sorrow turned to tremendous joy. Our joy may not come this morning or tomorrow morning or even the morning after that. We face too many hardships, too many difficult situations, too much sorrow here on earth to think joy will arrive with each morning. But it will come. God has promised: there will be a joyful morning for all who trust in him.

Jean Syswerda and Ann Spangler

God loves us so lavishly and outlandishly that our blessings in life are too numerous to count—if we have eyes to see. But no human being, be she eight or eighty, has only good days. The good news is that the most incredible best that is yet to come is beyond even our incredible imagination!

Marilyn Meberg

If we had no winter; the spring would not be so pleasant; if we did not sometimes taste of adversity, prosperity would not be so welcome.

Anne Bradstreet

For every single thing that has happened in our lives, we can learn to say with confidence, even with joy, "Not my will, but yours be done." This means saying yes to the happy and beautiful gifts, but also to the child you lost, the husband who never showed up, the breast cancer, the lost opportunities, the broken dreams, the endless list of human suffering. I do embrace the mystery that, in the darkest valleys the Light of the world is with us, and we will come to know him, to love and trust him, in ways we never have before.

Sheila Walsh

How much lighter trials become when we realize God's grace is twofold. It is not only the happy ending. It is also the peace we can feel during a painful journey, when we trust in God— all the way.

Doris Haase

Hope is a very tangible thing. The meaning of hope isn't just some flimsy wishing. It's a firm confidence in God's promises—that he will ultimately set things right.

Sheila Walsh

Hope that is seen is no hope at all. Who hopes
for what he already has? But if we hope for what we
do not yet have, we wait for it patiently.

ROMANS 8:24–25

Half-Baked

I'd had my Easter menu planned for weeks. Out of town company would fill our dining room to overflowing, so I'd decided to serve a turkey. Plenty of side dishes, too. And desserts? There would be so many you could make a meal on sweets if you wanted to.

I put the turkey in the oven at breakfast time, to give it a chance to pre-cook, and turned my attention to the side dishes and desserts. Midway through the morning, my husband asked, "Is the turkey in yet? I don't smell it cooking." Hmmmm. My nose didn't make out the familiar scent of roast turkey, either. Had I forgotten to turn the oven on?

No. It was worse than that. My oven had chosen that exact morning to die, right there on the spot. Company would be coming any minute, expecting to put the finishing touches on an Easter feast, and all I could offer them was half-baked poultry.

Ultimately, the Colonel at KFC bailed us out on the hot food items, but the rest of the side dishes and desserts consisted of variations on a Jell-O theme. Yet God took my ruined plans and gave us something better: a lot less clean up, a lot more fellowship, and a lot of laughter when that half-baked bird became our Easter centerpiece.

Sarah Hupp

An Unfolding Story

Elimelech, Naomi's husband, died, and she was left with her two sons. They married Moabite women, one named Orpah and the other Ruth. After they had lived there about ten years, both Mahlon and Kilion also died, and Naomi was left without her two sons and her husband.... So Naomi returned from Moab accompanied by Ruth the Moabitess, her daughter-in-law, arriving in Bethlehem as the barley harvest was beginning....

Boaz announced to the elders and all the people, "Today you are witnesses that I have bought from Naomi all the property of Elimelech, Kilion and Mahlon. I have also acquired Ruth the Moabitess, Mahlon's widow, as my wife, in order to maintain the name of the dead with his property, so that his name will not disappear from among his family or from the town records. Today you are witnesses!"...

So Boaz took Ruth and she became his wife. Then he went to her, and the LORD enabled her to conceive, and she gave birth to a son. The women said to Naomi: "Praise be to the LORD, who this day has not left you without a kinsman-redeemer. May he become famous throughout Israel! He will renew your life and sustain you in your old age. For your daughter-in-law, who loves you and who is better to you than seven sons, has given him birth."

Then Naomi took [Ruth's] child, laid him in her lap and cared for him. The women living there said, "Naomi has a son." And they named him Obed.

RUTH 1:3–5, 22; 4:9–10, 13–17

After so long an absence, Naomi's return created a great commotion in the town, and all the women welcomed her, saying, "Can this be Naomi?"

"Don't call me Naomi," she told them. "Call me Mara [meaning 'bitter'], because the Almighty has made my life very bitter. I went away full, but the Lord has brought me back empty."

Naomi could not see past her suffering. Like many of us, she may have felt her tragedies were punishment for her sins. Yet had she known the blessings yet in store, she might not have felt so hopeless. Instead, she might have compared herself to the tree that Job so graciously describes: "There is hope for a tree: If it is cut down, it will sprout again, and its new shoots will not fail. Its roots may grow old in the ground and its stump die in the soil, yet at the scent of water it will bud and put forth shoots like a plant" (Job 14:7–9).

Though she didn't know it, the scent of water was in the air. Naomi's life was beginning again, her story still unfolding. And so is yours.

Ann Spangler and Jean Syswerda

Three Trees' Wisdom

A Tale of Three Trees is a traditional American folktale retold by Angela Hunt. It's a wonderful story about what happens to three trees that each have their own special dreams. The first tree wanted to become the most beautiful treasure chest in the world, inlaid with jewels, carrying precious gold. It became the manger that rocked the Christ child. The second tree wanted to be the strongest sailing ship in the world. It became the boat that carried Jesus and his friends through a storm. The third tree never wanted to be cut down. It dreamed of growing to be the tallest tree in the world, a tree so magnificent that those who looked at it would give thanks to God. It became the cross on which Jesus gave his life.

Not one of the trees ended up living the life they had imagined. Their dreams were so grand, yet God's plans were greater—even though it meant a surrendering of personal dreams and an experience of such raw pain.

I cannot begin to grasp the ways of God. My only hope is to know the heart of God, and to keep on walking.

Sheila Walsh

Dolphin Perspective

A while back, I watched a nature special on TV about sick dolphins. The dolphins were dying. They could be saved if they could be treated with antibiotics. They had to be caught in huge nets, snatched up from the ocean, and then pulled overboard into waiting boats.

It must have been terrifying for them. Human hands were all over them. Human voices were shouting directions. They had no way of knowing that these new experiences were well-intentioned. They had only dolphin perspective. They were at Point A. Their very survival depended on them getting to Point C. But first they had to go through Point B—an insecure place full of unknowns, a place where endurance seemed impossible.

Life is difficult with limited perspective. At Point B our human perspective cannot anticipate the good possibilities of Point C. God's perspective sees the whole picture. He knows that to survive spiritually, we must experience transitional periods; we must go through Point B to get to Point C. Like the marine scientists who cared for the well-being of the dolphins, God has our best interests in mind through the whole painful process of change.

Valerie Bell

*Set your hearts on things above, where Christ is seated
at the right hand of God. Set your minds on things above,
not on earthly things. For you died, and your life is now
hidden with Christ in God. When Christ, who is your life,
appears, then you also will appear with him in glory.*

COLOSSIANS 3:1–4

*I heard a loud voice from the throne [of heaven] saying,
"Now the dwelling of God is with men, and he will live with
them. They will be his people, and God himself will be with them
and be their God. He will wipe every tear from their eyes. There
will be no more death or mourning or crying or pain, for the
old order of things has passed away." He who was seated
on the throne said, "I am making everything new!"*

REVELATION 21:3–5

What happens to us when we find ourselves in the middle of dark situation? Do we believe the things that are happening to us are accidental? Do we seek to change our circumstances, or do we accept them with a fatalistic attitude?

Sometimes we *can* change things, and we *must* try. That is why we are there! At other times, having tried, we find we cannot alter anything, nor can we escape, and so we must allow those situations to change us and we must accept the privilege of shining there.

Jill Briscoe

We need to be "shaken" off from every other foundation in order that we may be forced to rest on the foundation of God alone. This explains the necessity for those "shakings" through which so many Christians seem called to pass. The Lord sees that they are building their spiritual houses on flimsy foundations, which will not be able to withstand the storms of life; and not in anger but in tenderest love, he shakes our earth and our heaven until all that can be shaken is removed,… in order that only that which "cannot be shaken" may remain.

Hannah Whitall Smith

Simon's Lesson

The movie *Simon Birch* tells the story of a boy who is born with severe abnormalities. He is tiny, his best friend carries him around in a small basket attached to his bike, and his parents, perhaps out of superstition or fear, reject him. But Simon is a boy with an acute sense of destiny. He knows that God has put him on earth for a reason, and he is determined to fulfill his purpose.

Simon believes that God has called him to be a hero. Everyone looks at him and laughs, but it doesn't matter to Simon because there is a stronger melody playing in his spirit. And then his heroic moment comes. When he is just twelve years old, he dies saving the lives of a school bus full of children.

Simon saw clearly that this life we cling to, frantically squeezing every ounce of pleasure out of it as if we are dying of thirst, is not "it." Simon had lived his life, fulfilled his God-given mission, and now he was home. He knew that his life on earth was just the beginning.

Sheila Walsh

Those who hope in the LORD
  will renew their strength.
They will soar on wings like eagles;
  they will run and not grow weary,
they will walk and not be faint.

ISAIAH 40:31

Isaiah 40 tells us soaring like an eagle through the currents of life is God's flight plan for us. We start out the trip by waiting on him. We learn to trust. Then we spread our wings and flap them. The result? We rise up and fall down, rise and fall, as we ride the currents. It looks effortless, and in many ways it is. Of course, were we not pushed into flight by our Father, we might never get beyond just waiting. God sets up circumstances that push us into trusting him to hold us up. It's the only way.

Barbara Johnson

God Intends Good

Satan plans to hinder the work of an effective missionary by arranging for him to trip in the jungle and break a leg; God allows the accident so that the missionary's godly response to pain and discomfort will bring glory to God. Satan brews a hurricane to kill thousands in a small village in Bangladesh; God uses the storm to display his awesome power, to drive some to search for him. Satan schemed that a seventeen-year-old girl named Joni would break her neck, hoping to ruin her life; God sent the broken neck in answer to her prayer for a closer walk with him.

As a friend once said, "God sends things, but Satan often brings them. Praise God that when Satan causes calamity, we can answer him with the words that Joseph answered his brothers with when they sold him into slavery, 'You intended to harm me, but God intended it for good' (Genesis 50:20)."

Joni Eareckson Tada

How priceless is your unfailing love!
Both high and low among men
   find refuge in the shadow of your wings, O Lord.
PSALM 36:7

The Lord will rescue me from every evil attack
and will bring me safely to his heavenly kingdom.
   To him be glory for ever and ever. Amen.
2 TIMOTHY 4:18

Surely goodness and love will follow me
   all the days of my life,
   and I will dwell in the house of the LORD
   forever.
PSALM 23:6

A Perfect Timetable

Fifteen years ago I had cancer and was told I might not live out the year. Of course that was bad news. The worst! But then I had this epiphany: If I'm going to die anyway, why not die happy? Why not indulge myself with chocolate to my heart's content?

With that in mind, I began to eat great quantities of milk chocolate. Every day of my life, for over fifteen years, I've eaten the equivalent of six to eight Hershey bars. I say "equivalent" because sometimes it's frozen Snickers Bars or a fudge binge. Debbie, who owns the fudge shop at the Farmer's Market, asks, "Having a lot of company again?" when she takes my money and hands me three pounds of fudge. *Well, noooo, not exactly.*

I'm no brain, but go figure! *Chocolate is the cure for cancer!* A study was made using male graduates from an Ivy League university. It revealed that those who ate chocolate lived nearly a year longer than those who didn't.

The bottom line here is that regardless of modern science, God has a timetable for our lives. If I had died as the doctor predicted, I never would have witnessed my daughter Mindy's graduation from high school, or seen her in her prom dress, or taken pictures of her as homecoming princess. I would have missed my daughter Dana's graduation from college; missed seeing her fall head-over-heels for Barry. I would not have had the chance to help her plan her wedding, or help Wayne hang wallpaper in our new house. I never would have written a book—the outgrowth of the journal I kept about having cancer, chemotherapy, and reconstructive surgery. And I never would have had a chance to meet all my wonderful new "old" friends because of my speaking engagements. I'm thankful that God is in charge!

Dear Lord, Don't let me become frantic when I hear the statistics. The computer doesn't know me—doesn't know how much I laugh and cry, how well I'm loved, who my friends are, or how I'm prayed for. It certainly doesn't know that you have a timetable for my life and your timing is perfect. Amen.

Sue Buchanan

Nahum 1:7 says, "The LORD is good." He is good for he is God. As God, he has custom-designed a plan for our lives. He works in our trouble so that good will come out of it.

He becomes a stronghold for us in the time of our trouble. He becomes our place of security and safety. God is a stronghold to those who trust him. He will never fail you, forsake you or forget you.

Millie Stamm

I'm always amazed at God's hand. So present. So comforting. He is my home. He is my family. He is my friend. Every situation, every circumstance—he proves himself true. Never a want without him knowing. Never a desire without him seeing. Never a need without him coming to meet it. He will. His way. He promises.

Kathy Troccoli

Those people who ponder, and meditate, and weigh the affairs of life—how much more joyful would be their lives, if they would take their experiences, day by day, and lift them up and praise God for them.

Lettie Cowman

One of the things I learned about skiing is that no matter how good you get at it, you still fall, you still get hurt; you have good days and bad days. But ask any skier, and he or she will tell you it's the ride of your life. I am learning this about the rest of my life a little bit every day. Life is not the way I want it to be a lot of the time, but I do believe that pushing through my fear and heading down the mountain is the only way to live. I wanted it to be easier than this. It's not. Saying yes to God is much more difficult than I thought it would be. But it's also exhilarating.

Sheila Walsh

> *God knows, not I, the reason why*
> *His winds of storm drive through my door;*
> *I am content to live or die*
> *Just knowing this, nor knowing more.*
> *My Father's hand appointing me*
> *My days and ways, so I am free.*

Margaret Sangster

My frame was not hidden from you
when I was made in the secret place.
When I was woven together in the depths of the earth,
your eyes saw my unformed body.
All the days ordained for me
were written in your book
before one of them came to be.
How precious to me are your thoughts, O God!
How vast is the sum of them!
Were I to count them,
they would outnumber the grains of sand.

PSALM 139:15–18

Laughing With the Lord

Are you going through a difficult struggle? Sit down and hold God's gift of grace in your lap. Slowly untie the ribbons. Now remove the lid on the box. Reach beneath the tissue paper. It's party time! In the middle of your trial, God has prepared a celebration. Jesus triumphed over the worst, and now he will help you to do the same.

How will he do it? In a way you didn't expect. Jesus knows about everything you're going through, and he has made arrangements for you to look back on it—and laugh. He is going to bring laughter and liberty into your circumstances. Wherever Jesus is, there's a party going on.

No, life won't ever be perfect. Even in the land of milk and honey you can get kicked by a cow or stung by a bee. But when that happens, you can laugh with the Lord by your side and say with him, "Been there. Done that!" Embrace grace.

Barbara Johnson

Since prayer is simply talking to God, why not talk to him about the very thing that causes our blood pressure to go up in the daytime, and sleep to elude us at night? First Thessalonians 5:17 says, "pray continually." This seems like an impossible task until we realize that God wants us to talk with him at all times about all things.

Lisa Fort

Believe me, we've all had our prayers answered in ways we didn't particularly like. But as the years go by, I have learned that "getting what we want" is not nearly as rewarding as the personal relationship available to us with the One who is listening to our requests.

Chonda Pierce

Sad soul, take comfort nor forget
The sunrise never failed us yet.
CELIA THAXTER

When our relationship with God is intact, there is always a settled peace. Relationship—that's the key. There is no substitute for the peace that a relationship with Christ offers. And where there is peace, laughter abounds!

Moving to an intimate walk with the Lord through the power of the Holy Spirit helps us find the fun—even after the darkest days.

Chonda Pierce

Jesus said, "Now is your time of grief, but I will see you again and you will rejoice, and no one will take away your joy."

JOHN 16:22

Noticing Something Beautiful

"When the LORD saw that Leah was not loved, he opened her womb" (Genesis 29:31).The Lord *noticed* Leah's misery. The God of Abraham, Isaac, and Jacob (Leah's husband) looked down and saw a woman who was lonely and sad because her husband loved his other wife better than he loved her. So, to ease her sorrow, to provide her comfort, God gave her children— beautiful, upright, strong children, one of whom would found the lineage of the priests of Israel and another who was an ancestor of Jesus himself.

This same God of Abraham, Isaac, Jacob, and Leah is our God. He sees our miseries, no matter how small or how large. He knows our circumstances, our feelings, our hurts. And, just as in Leah's life, he's willing to step in and create something beautiful in and through us.

Jean Syswerda and Ann Spangler

The Spirit of the Sovereign LORD is on me,
because the LORD has anointed me
to preach good news to the poor.
He has sent me to bind up the brokenhearted,
to proclaim freedom for the captives
and release from darkness for the prisoners . . .
to comfort all who mourn,
and provide for those who grieve in Zion—
to bestow on them a crown of beauty
instead of ashes,
the oil of gladness
instead of mourning,
and a garment of praise
instead of a spirit of despair.
They will be called oaks of righteousness,
a planting of the LORD
for the display of his splendor.

ISAIAH 61:1–3

Singing Through Tears

When I was a teenager I sang in a trio that traveled all over West Virginia and beyond. Once we had driven for miles to sing at a youth banquet in a dank, drab, crepe-paper-draped church basement. While we were rehearsing, trying to get used to the ancient, out-of-tune, beat-up old piano, we couldn't help noticing a teenage boy sobbing like his heart was broken. Those around him were making an effort, but no one seemed to be able to console him.

We were seated, the blessing was said, and there was a pall-like silence. At last the kitchen door gave a great "whoosh," and through it came a very determined-looking woman balancing the biggest platter you've ever seen.

On it was ... the biggest ... the biggest ... what? Let's just say it was the biggest *bird of unknown origin* we'd ever seen. It was practically meatless; its ribs stood out like a snow fence on a winter's day, and the puddle it reclined in contained more grease than Elvis Presley's pompadour. With great ceremony, the platter was placed on the head table in front of us, and carved right under our noses!

Only moments before our trio was introduced someone came forward and gave a lovely speech, thanking the selfless young man for contributing his pet 4-H blue-ribbon goose to the youth dinner! There was a round of applause, and it was time for us to sing.

"Some glad morning when this life is o'er . . . !" The words were barely out of our mouths when we remembered the very inappropriate next line of the song! What could we do? It was too late to go back!

"I'll fly away," we sang to a fresh round of tears.

Fortunately, sometimes you can't tell the difference between laughing and crying. Our bodies were shaking convulsively all the way through our first number. Tears were running down our faces like rivers. Afterward everyone thanked us for being so sensitive and caring. They thought our ill-chosen song was a tribute!

And just think! God loves to hear his children sing. It's music to his ears, and it brings him glory. He loves the sound of your voice in praise, too. How long has it been since he has heard it?

Sue Buchanan

Stressed Spelled Backward Is Desserts!

Stressed Out

I overheard two five-year-olds talking. The first said, "I'm stressed out!"

The second said, "You can't be stressed out. That's only for grown-ups!"

Sure enough, the accent may be on youth these days, but the stress is on adults. Always reflecting on the things we haven't done, we start each day worrying earlier and stay up later to worry every night.

Yet some of us are learning that cares are the tools God uses to fashion us for better things. He uses reverses to move us forward. Reverses and cares bow us down low until we finally drop to our knees. But a lot of kneeling keeps us in good standing because it brings us closer to God. Being close to God, we find peace.

Even if our cares aren't resolved as we wish and even if we finally have to admit life in this world will never be safe or predictable, we may discover that's because we were made for another place. So, don't get stressed out; get blessed out!

Barbara Johnson

In my distress I called to the L ORD *;*
I called out to my God.
From his temple he heard my voice;
my cry came to his ears.

2 SAMUEL 22:7

Praise be to the Lord, to God our Savior,
who daily bears our burdens.

PSALM 68:19

L ORD *, you establish peace for us;*
all that we have accomplished you have done for us.

ISAIAH 26:12

I need to slow down. And I'm asking the Lord to help me do it. I want to move slowly enough to be aware of all the joys he has hidden for me. I want to slow down enough to grow as he wants me to grow. I want to be quiet enough to hear his voice. I need his wisdom to know how to spend my time and how to order my days. I need to slow down.

Kathryn Hillen

Want to lift your spirits from the hustle and bustle of the day? Sing to the Lord. When praises go up, blessings come down. Now, isn't that something to sing about?

Thelma Wells

In life we experience many losses. A wise woman will focus on the small blessings of her life as a way of loving her life and keeping her losses in perspective. Learn to appreciate what you cannot lose: the air, the sun, the love of God, a constant friend, and a new day. Nurture a contented soul.

Valerie Bell

One-Way Street

One Christmas I wanted to make a card for my friend Mary Graham to commemorate the season in a special way. She had just returned from a mission trip to Russia, so I drew a Russian Orthodox church on the front of the card. Under it I planned to write "Merry Christmas" in Russian. But when I searched my books, the library, dictionaries, etc., I could not find out how to say "Merry Christmas" in that language.

I didn't give up. I found a short Russian word followed by a long one (looked like Merry Christmas to me!) and used them. I added this note to the card:

"I wanted this to say Merry Christmas in Russian, but I couldn't find it. So it says One-Way Street, which is sort of the same thing. The birth of Christ is the One Way to peace, hope, joy, laughter ... and all that Christmas means. May Christmas be a one-way street to happiness."

We've had so much fun with that card. And on blustery December days we smile at total strangers and say with a big grin, "One-Way Street!"

Luci Swindoll

When God says he has given us all things to enjoy, I don't think he's talking just about the grandeur of mountains, sunsets, and waterfalls. It's anything that gives us pleasure and is in accordance with his will. So, I don't want to allow the demands of life to blind me to the little joys that pop up every day. Appreciating those little joys frequently provides the stamina for the big demands.

Marilyn Meberg

I collect laughs like others collect marbles or butterflies. It works like this ... sometimes while I'm sitting on a plane, I will think of something that made me laugh once before, and I laugh again. And then again on another day, maybe when I'm walking through a grocery store or filling the dishwasher.

Maybe you can start your own collection of laughs. Remember, there is no childproof cap on this bottle. And there are unlimited refills. So when was the last time you had a good laugh? It's time to take your medicine.

Chonda Pierce

An Eager Comforter

When God met Hannah at the temple in Shiloh, he not only answered her prayer for a child, he answered her prayer for comfort in her misery. He gave her consolation in her disappointment and strength to face her situation. Scripture does not say that she went away sure she would bear a child, but it does make it clear that she went away comforted: "Her face was no longer downcast" (1 Samuel 1:18). What even the love and care of her husband, Elkanah, could not provide, God could provide.

God is willing to meet us just as he met Hannah. Whatever our distress, whatever hard situations we face, he is willing—more than that—he is eager to meet our needs and give us his grace and comfort. No other person—not our husband, not our closest friends, not our parents, not our children—can render the relief and support and encouragement that our God has waiting for us.

Jean Syswerda and Ann Spangler

You will keep in perfect peace
  him whose mind is steadfast,
  because he trusts in you.
Trust in the LORD forever,
  for the LORD, the LORD, is the Rock eternal.
    ISAIAH 26:3–4

I will listen to what God the LORD will say;
  he promises peace to his people.
    PSALM 85:8

The apostles gathered around Jesus and reported to him all they had
done and taught. Then, because so many people were coming and
going that they did not even have a chance to eat, he said to them,
  "Come with me by yourselves to a quiet place and get some rest."
    MARK 6:30–31

  "I will refresh the weary and satisfy the faint," says the LORD.
    JEREMIAH 31:25

Many times I've asked God for something specific, and he's dropped it in my lap; but because it didn't look like what I thought it should, I turned it down. *Forget that, Lord,* I say. *You've gotta be kidding.* God doesn't kid. He's the master of creativity, if I just trust him on that.

Luci Swindoll

It's so easy to forget everything God's already done by being preoccupied with what you want him to do right here, right now. By forgetting his blessings, you form a habit of ingratitude. By frequently thanking God for what he's done, you build a habit of gratitude, which will also deepen your trust in God's compassion, mercy, faithfulness, and power.... Build your confidence in God. Form a habit of remembrance. Keep God's faithfulness in the forefront of your heart.

Ann Spangler and Jean Syswerda

Thankfulness takes the sting out of life by focusing away from loss to those blessings which remain.

Valerie Bell

It Makes Me Mad

Very few of us celebrate God all day, every day as Philippians 4:4 implies we should.

We used to have a neighbor whose outlook on life was less than rosy; her proverbial cup was always half empty. It hadn't been *her day* for as long as we could remember, and she wouldn't recognize a joke if it was lit up in neon.

On what seemed to be the most perfect day of the year, several of us gathered for a cup of coffee. "This day just makes me mad," she announced for all to hear. You could hear a pin drop. We were baffled. "Why in the world does it make you mad?" we asked. "'Cause I know it's not going to last."

Celebrating God all day, every day is a real challenge! It's a challenge, but it's do-able. Maybe not all at once, but maybe we can start small and sneak up on it! Maybe try it once a week, then twice a week, then once a day and finally *all day, every day.* I'll try if you will!

Sue Buchanan

My Toilet Overfloweth

I was scheduled to speak at a ladies' Bible study, so I had dressed appropriately—pantyhose, heels, silk suit—the works. Because my mother had always reminded me to "Go to the bathroom before you leave the house," I decided I'd better follow her admonition now, too. That chore accomplished, I began to inch my pantyhose evenly over my knees as I flushed the toilet. That's when I knew I was in trouble.

The powder room toilet had been acting up over the last few weeks, sometimes refusing to shut off. I had been assured that the problem would be resolved on Saturday, but today was *Friday*, and that old toilet was threatening to overflow.

With my pantyhose riding at knee height, I quickly hiked my silk skirt up over my navel, jammed my jacket hem into the skirt's bulge, (so that the suit wouldn't be in my way!), and reached across the burbling toilet bowl to yank the lid off the tank reservoir.

But, I was moments too late. The water had crested the top of the bowl and began to spill onto the surrounding tile floor, splashing all over me.

To stop the cantankerous toilet's overflow, I had to peel off my jacket, slip out of my blouse, hold those pieces of clothing in my teeth, and plunge my arm deep into the icy tank to close the shut off valve. By the time I finished the task, my heels, pantyhose, and silk suit were soaked with the splashings of toilet water.

For a quick $10,000 from one of those funny video shows, someone should have been standing behind me in that tiny powder room. The view of a drenched, half-clad woman fighting an overflowing toilet was beyond comical—it was hysterical. Just imagining that camera crew made me laugh.

I changed out of my wet things and arrived at the Bible study in a less-than-perfect outfit. But the delicious retelling of my experience reminded us all that we have a choice in how we respond to the things that God allows to come our way. We can rant and rave, complain and curse, or we can allow God's Spirit to fill us with joy—a joy that will overflow and splash on others—just like my cantankerous toilet!

Sarah Hupp

I have discovered time and time again in my life that talking to God is always "timely." Discerning his Spirit and what he would have us learn and do in any situation is easiest when we simply ask him and then trust him to be on time. I always want to be prepared and strive to do my best in every performance, retreat, or encounter. But there are times when our best is not enough. We must trust the Holy Spirit to take our best and make it better. I want to be funny when the time is right. But I also want to be silent when the time is right, trusting God to fill in the gaps. In the tough times or the fun times, God is still God, and we need to draw ever closer to him.

Chonda Pierce

How will we ever break through the fear that consumes us if we cannot pour it out in its rawest form at the throne of grace? Where else will we go if we can't knock, knock, knock on heaven's door?

Sheila Walsh

May the Lord of peace himself give you peace
at all times and in every way.
2 THESSALONIANS 3:16

Trust in the LORD with all your heart
and lean not on your own understanding;
in all your ways acknowledge him,
and he will make your paths straight.
PROVERBS 3:5–6

The LORD will guide you always;
he will satisfy your needs in a sun-scorched land
and will strengthen your frame.
You will be like a well-watered garden,
like a spring whose waters never fail.
ISAIAH 58:11

Commit to the LORD whatever you do,
and your plans will succeed.
PROVERBS 16:3

Dream a Heavenly Dream

What is your dream? What do you deeply desire? Could it be that those desires have been planted in your heart by the heavenly Father? Do you believe he has a purpose for your most cherished dream because it originated with him? God wants you to pursue the talents he has created within you. He means for them to blossom through your personality. Your availability makes it happen.

How do you keep believing, keep the faith, keep the spiritual workout up? By knowing God hasn't given up on you! He has never lost faith. He sees the dream in your heart as bright as the lights on a Broadway marquee. Not one ounce of his enthusiasm for your talents has dissipated.

It also helps to know that God is big enough to handle your doubts, slumps, and temper tantrums. He is staying in your court. He isn't going to drop the ball in your game of life. And he is your biggest fan!

Barbara Johnson

My husband, David Pierce, doesn't use the word *adversity*. What some may think as an impossible situation, he shrugs his shoulders and says, "Okay, what are our options?" He gathers strength for the day and plows through. And he laughs.

Chonda Pierce

When you get into a tight place and everything goes against you until it seems as though you could not hold on a minute longer; never give up, for that is just the place and time that the tide will turn.

Harriet Beecher Stowe

The Lord miraculously puts everything into his perspective when my mind and heart are set on all that he is, on all that he's done, on all that he's promised. I become more thankful, more hopeful, and most importantly, I am humbled. His love is never-ending. Look, listen, and hear. God is near. He will bring you perfect peace.

Kathy Troccoli

A Cup for the Coffee

We were made to contain the very life of Jesus. He means to live out the reality of who he is right here within the reality of who we are. He means to be our lives—the breath in our lungs, the thoughts in our heads, the energy and creativity in our jobs, the love in our hearts. He means to take on the stress and unravel the inner complications so that we can move through our lives just as he did, in gentleness and simplicity and harmony.

We were never intended to be more than containers. We are the glove; he is the hand. We are the cup; he is the coffee. We are the lamp; he is the light.

This is what we were made for. This is the intended purpose of the human person and personality; not to be gods, but to contain God. This is the sheer simplicity of God's design that was shattered by humanity's sin. And it is the reason that Jesus came and cared and was killed and laid in a tomb and raised to life again ... so that he could give us another shot at being what we were intended to be.

Claire Cloninger

"Have faith in God," Jesus answered. "I tell you the truth, if anyone says to this mountain, 'Go, throw yourself into the sea,' and does not doubt in his heart but believes that what he says will happen, it will be done for him. Therefore I tell you, whatever you ask for in prayer, believe that you have received it, and it will be yours."

MARK 11:22–24

Why are you downcast, O my soul?
Why so disturbed within me?
Put your hope in God,
for I will yet praise him,
my Savior and my God.

PSALM 43:5

Oh, that we could reason less about our troubles, and sing and praise more! There are thousands of things that we wear as shackles which we might use as instruments with music in them, if we only knew how.

Lettie Cowman

It's so simple! God is totally trustworthy, and I can relax in his plans. And besides that, all he wants is—are you ready for this?— for me to be his person. *Just be his person!* I don't have to be brilliant or have a theology degree. *Just be his person, for heaven's sake!* Wow!

Sue Buchanan

I began to seek the Lord with all my heart, asking him what he had in mind for my life. I found peace quickly as I sought the Lord's plan for my life. I asked the Lord to place me where I would fit in and where I was needed. Right now the only career goal I have is to be living the plans God has for me, to be seeking him with all my heart. Are you?

Sue Richards

The life of the apostle Paul consisted of much traveling and a very irregular schedule. His body consequently received little rest. Paul often encountered misunderstanding and suspicion.

God the Father, however, knew what his child needed. He comforted Paul through the person of Titus. Titus was in a cheerful mood when he visited Paul. Their time together turned out to be spiritually and physically refreshing to Paul.

The sense of rest that one person can convey to another can hardly be overestimated. People need one another, not only in important things such as functioning in society, church and the home, but also in small things such as when feeling discouraged or depressed. We cannot do without one another. We are privileged when we have friends who meet such needs.

Gien Karssen

Practicing Love

"Love is patient, love is kind," are some of the most beautiful words I know. They speak of the giving dimension of love, a lifestyle of graciousness, both of small graces and of the deeper offerings of the soul. "Love is patient, love is kind," runs the gamut of the kindness scale, from a simple, yet appropriate word in passing, when peevishness might have been in order, to the sharing of life on the most intimate connected levels, day after day and year after year. It suggests a consistent, predictable offering of grace, a lifestyle of kind gestures and words, whether given to another for only a second or for a lifetime in the extended day-by-day togetherness of life.

How bleak this world would be without those who practice small kindnesses, small loves. Worse yet—how desperate this world would be without those who know how to give from their souls, who walk through dark places with others, who comfort, who cheer, who connect, who hang in there no matter what.

Valerie Bell

ACKNOWLEDGMENTS

Bell, Valerie. *A Well-Tended Soul: Staying Beautiful for the Rest of Your Life.* Grand Rapids, MI: Zondervan, 1996. Used by permission.

Buchanan, Sue. *Duh-Votions: Words of Wisdom for the Spiritually Challenged.* Grand Rapids, MI: Zondervan, 1999. Used by permission.

Carter, Norvella, Ph.D., ed. *Women to Women: Perspective of Fifteen African-American Christian Women.* Grand Rapids, MI: Zondervan, 1996. Used by permission.

Clairmont, Patsy; Barbara Johnson, Marilyn Meberg, Luci Swindoll, Sheila Walsh, Thelma Wells. *Boundless Love.* Grand Rapids, MI: Zondervan, 2001. Used by permission.
Extravagant Grace. Grand Rapids, MI: Zondervan, 2000. Used by permission.
Outrageous Joy. Grand Rapids, MI: Zondervan, 1999. Used by permission.
Overjoyed! Grand Rapids, MI: Zondervan, 1999. Used by permission.

Draper, Edythe. *Draper's Book of Quotations for the Christian World.* Wheaton, IL: Tyndale House Publishers, Inc., 1992.

Hosier, Helen. *The Quotable Christian: Favorite Quotes from Notable Christians.* Urichsville, OH: Barbour Publishing, Inc., 1998. Used by permission.

Hupp, Sarah M. *Trust in the Lord.* White Plains, NY: Peter Pauper Press, 1999. Used by permission.

More of God's Words of Life for Women. Grand Rapids, MI: Zondervan, 2000. Used by permission.

NIV Classics Devotional Bible. Grand Rapids, MI: Zondervan, 1996. Used by permission.

NIV Seniors' Devotional Bible. Grand Rapids, MI: Zondervan, 1996. Used by permission.

NIV Women's Devotional Bible 2. Grand Rapids, MI: Zondervan, 1995. Used by permission.

Pierce, Chonda. *It's Always Darkest Before the Fun Comes Up.* Grand Rapids, MI: Zondervan, 1998. Used by permission.

Spangler, Ann, and Jean E. Syswerda. *Women of the Bible: A One-Year Devotional Study of Women in Scripture.* Grand Rapids, MI: Zondervan, 1999. Used by permission.

Troccoli, Kathy. *My Life Is in Your Hands.* Grand Rapids, MI: Zondervan, 1997. Used by permission.

Walsh, Sheila. *Living Fearlessly.* Grand Rapids, MI: Zondervan, 2001. Used by permission.